Jobs if You Like...

History

Charlotte Guillain

Heinemann
LIBRARY
Chicago, Illinois

www.capstonepub.com

Visit our website to find out more information about Heinemann-Raintree books.

To order:

☎ Phone 800-747-4992

🖳 Visit www.capstonepub.com to browse our catalog and order online.

Edited by Rebecca Rissman, Daniel Nunn, and Adrian Vigliano
Designed by Steve Mead
Picture research by Elizabeth Alexander
Originated by Capstone Global Library
Printed and bound in China by South China Printing Company

16 15 14 13 12
10 9 8 7 6 5 4 3 2 1

Library of Congress Cataloging-in-Publication Data
Guillain, Charlotte.
   History / Charlotte Guillain.
      p. cm.—(Jobs if you like...)
   Includes bibliographical references and index.
   ISBN 978-1-4329-6807-6 (hb)—ISBN 978-1-4329-6818-2 (pbk.) 1. History—Vocational guidance—Juvenile literature. 2. Occupations—Juvenile literature. 3. Professions—Juvenile literature. I. Title.
   D16.19.G85 2012
   902.3—dc23   2011031927

Acknowledgments
We would like to thank the following for permission to reproduce photographs: Alamy pp. 4 (© National Geographic Image Collection), 14 (© PhotoStock-Israel), 17 (© Expuesto - Nicolas Randall), 20 (© France Chateau), 24 (© Barry Mason), 26 (© B.O'Kane); Corbis pp. 5 (© Robert Schlesinger/dpa), 6 © Luke MacGregor/Reuters), 8 © Handout/Reuters), 9 © Mahmoud illean / Demotix/Demotix), 11 © Peter Steffen/dpa), 12 © Everett Kennedy Brown/epa), 15 © Dave Bartruff), 25 © Pascal Deloche/Godong); Getty Images pp. 7 (Sarah L. Voisin/The Washington Post), 10 (Peter Macdiarmid), 13 (Margaret Thomas/The Washington Post), 16 (Miguel Medina/AFP), 18 (Raphael Gaillarde/Gamma-Rapho), 19 (Francois Guillot/AFP), 22 (Mike Clarke/AFP), 23 (Stan Honda/AFP), 27 (James Devaney/WireImage); Shutterstock p. 21 (© Nadejda Ivanova).

Cover photo of a reenactment of the Battle of Wittstock 1636 reproduced with permission of Corbis (© Robert Schlesinger/dpa).

Every effort has been made to contact copyright holders of material reproduced in this book. Any omissions will be rectified in subsequent printings if notice is given to the publisher.

Contents

Why Does History Matter? 4
Be a Museum Curator 6
Be an Archaeologist 8
Be a Conservator 10
Be a Costume Designer... 12
Be a Teacher 14
Be a Researcher 16
Be an Archivist 18
Be a Museum Educator... 20
Be an Auctioneer... 22
Be a Tour Guide.. 24
Choosing the Right Job for You 26
History Job Chart... 28
Glossary 30
Find Out More.. 31
Index.. 32

Some words are shown in bold, **like this**. You can find out what they mean by looking in the glossary.

Why Does History Matter?

Do you ever wonder why we learn history? History is more than just amazing stories from the past. When we study history, we learn why the world is the way it is today. We can also learn from mistakes people made in the past.

Animals that lived in the past are a part of history.

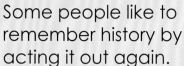
Some people like to
remember history by
acting it out again.

History can be very exciting. Many people like to
learn about history all their lives. Read this book to
find out about some great jobs that involve history.
Could one of them be for you?

Be a Museum Curator

If you like finding out about objects from the past, then maybe you could be a museum curator. Your job would be to get new **artifacts** for a museum. Sometimes you might trade artifacts with other museums.

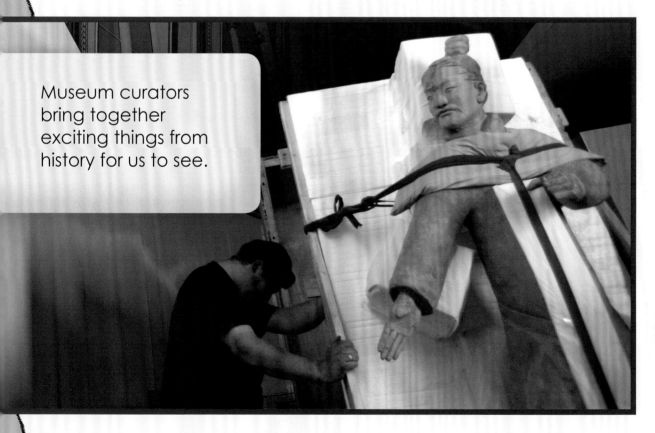

Museum curators bring together exciting things from history for us to see.

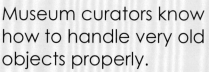
Museum curators have to organize all the objects in their museum so that visitors can understand them. They need to make sure the artifacts are looked after carefully. Sometimes they might talk to people about the objects in the museum.

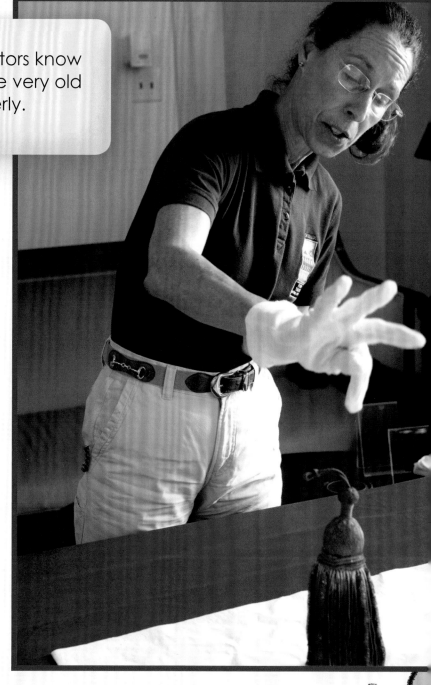

Be an Archaeologist

If you were an archaeologist, you would look for places where objects from history might be found. Then you would work with a team on an **excavation**. You would carefully dig up the ground and look for **artifacts** from history.

These archaeologists are digging up the remains of a pyramid in Egypt.

When archaeologists find artifacts, they clean and identify them. Sometimes they do tests in a **laboratory** to find out how old an artifact is. They might use computers to show how a place looked hundreds of years ago.

This archaeologist is looking closely at an artifact to find out more about it.

Be a Conservator

If you were a conservator, your job would be to look after art and objects from history. You would probably **specialize** in one type of object, such as sculptures, costumes, or paintings. You would work in a **laboratory**, as well as visit museums and **art galleries**.

A conservator knows how to clean a painting without damaging it.

Conservators know how to handle artifacts with care.

Conservators look at objects carefully to see if they are damaged. They make repairs and **preserve** objects to keep them in good condition. They make sure **artifacts** are kept in a safe place, where they won't be damaged.

Be a Costume Designer

If you love clothes and history, then maybe you could be a costume designer! When people set plays, television programs, or films in the past, they need the right costumes. A costume designer designs and makes clothes from history.

Costume designers know how clothes from history should look.

Costume designers draw their ideas after doing research.

Costume designers read the **script**, then they **research** the clothes people wore at that time in history. Then they sketch their ideas and talk to the other people working on the play or film. When everyone is happy, they make the clothes.

Be a Teacher

If you really love history, then a great job for you could be teaching. You would teach students about the world and how it has changed over time. You would help students to see how the past helps us make decisions about the future.

Sometimes history teachers take their classes on field trips.

Grade school teachers tell children how history fits in with everything else they learn at school. In high school, some teachers **specialize** in history. Teachers sometimes organize field trips to museums and other places to find out more about the past.

History teachers can take children on lots of fun trips!

Be a Researcher

If you were a researcher, it would be your job to find information and share it with people. You might do **research** for a television or radio program or for a company report. You would need to find the facts and check that they are correct.

Researchers might look at old film to find out about the past.

Researchers sometimes use very old books to do their work.

Researchers use libraries, museums, and the Internet to find information. Often, they have to find out about life in the past. Knowing about history helps them to find the facts they need and to write about this information in a clear way.

Be an Archivist

If you like reading as well as history, then maybe you could be an archivist. An archivist takes care of important **records** and documents from history. Some archivists take care of old books or maps, while others look after photographs, film, or sound files.

Archivists wear gloves so that they do not damage old books.

Archivists organize collections so that they can find documents.

Archivists make sure that collections are kept in a safe place. They organize the documents in the archive and help people to find and look at them. Sometimes archivists put the documents in their collection on the Internet so that many people can look at them.

19

Be a Museum Educator

If you were a museum educator, your job would be to talk to museum visitors. You would help people understand history by talking about it. You would also show them objects and explain what they were used for in the past.

Museum educators help to bring history to life.

Some museum educators organize activities for children visiting a museum or **art gallery**. These activities help children understand **exhibitions**. Museum educators might help children handle objects in the museum's collection.

Museum educators help visitors understand what life was like in the past.

Be an Auctioneer

If you were an **auctioneer**, you would look at **antiques** people wanted to sell. You would check the objects to see if they were in good condition. Then you would decide how much the objects might be worth.

Auctioneers need to know a lot about objects from history.

This painting is being sold at an auction.

Auctioneers give information to people who are thinking about buying an object. They hold an auction, where people can offer to buy the object. The person who offers the highest price gets the object.

Be a Tour Guide

If you were a tour guide, you might show people around a place or area that has an important history. Some tour guides show visitors around old buildings. Other tour guides take people around a city and tell them what happened there in the past.

A tour guide can show people the important places in a city.

Tour guides need to remember a lot of facts from history. They need to be good at talking to people about the past in an interesting way. They need to know a lot of information to answer people's questions.

Tour guides tell people interesting facts and stories.

Choosing the Right Job for You

When you decide what you want to do when you grow up, don't just think about school subjects. Think about what you enjoy doing. If you like talking to people, then you could be a museum educator or a tour guide.

If you're interested in clothes and art, then you could be a costume designer. There are so many exciting jobs using history that there is something to suit everyone.

Five things you couldn't do without history

- Be a good citizen
- Understand where your family and friends come from
- Learn from mistakes people made in the past
- Enjoy amazing stories about people in the past
- Understand why your world works the way it does

History Job Chart

If you want to find out more about any of the jobs in this book, start here:

	Archaeologist	Archivist	Auctioneer	Conservator	
You need to:	Be very careful and patient	Be careful and organized	Know what different **antiques** are worth	Know a lot about objects from history	
Best thing about it:	Discovering old and unusual objects!	Working with very old documents that not many people see!	Selling antiques for a big price!	Sharing amazing **artifacts** with many people!	

Costume designer	Museum curator	Museum educator	Researcher	Teacher	Tour guide
Be interested in fashion	Know a lot about historical objects	Be good at explaining history to people	Be good at finding information	Enjoy helping people to learn	Know a lot of information about a place
Seeing your costumes on the screen!	Seeing visitors enjoy your **exhibitions**!	Having fun sharing history with visitors!	Finding incredible facts about the past!	Seeing your pupils get excited about history!	Bringing history to life for people!

Glossary

antique object made a long time ago

auctioneer person who sells things at auctions

art gallery place where paintings and sculptures are displayed

artifact object made by people

excavation digging up of objects from history

exhibition place where pieces of art and artifacts are displayed for people to look at

laboratory place where research can be done on objects from the past

preserve keep something safe from damage

record written information

research find as much information about something as possible

script words that are spoken in a play, film, or television program

specialize focus on one particular area

Find Out More

Smithsonian Education
www.smithsonianeducation.org/students/explore_by_topic/history_culture.html
This Website of the Smithsonian Center for Education and Museum Studies will help you to find out more about history. There are also fun games and activities!

NPS Archaeology Program
www.nps.gov/archeology/public/kids/index.htm
Discover more about archaeology and what archaeologists do at this Website of the U.S. National Park Service.

American Colonial Clothing
www.history.org/history/clothing/intro/index.cfm
Find out more about clothing in America in the 1700s at this Website of Colonial Williamsburg. There's also an activity to dress a colonial person from head to toe!

Index

antiques 22, 28

archaeologists 8–9, 28

archivists 18–19, 28

art 10, 21, 27

art galleries 10, 21

artifacts 6, 7, 8–9, 11, 28

auctioneers 22–23, 28

children 14–15, 21

clothes 12, 13, 27

computers 9

conservators 10–11, 28

costume designers 12–13, 27, 29

documents 18–19, 28

excavations 8

exhibitions 21, 29

facts 16, 17, 25, 29

grade schools 15

high schools 15

importance 4, 27

Internet 17, 19

laboratories 9, 10

museum curators 6–7, 29

museum educators 20–21, 26, 29

museums 6–7, 10, 15, 17, 20, 21, 29

records 18–19

research 13, 16–17, 29

researchers 16–17, 29

teachers 14–15, 29

television 12, 16

tour guides 24–25, 26, 29